The United States

Delaware

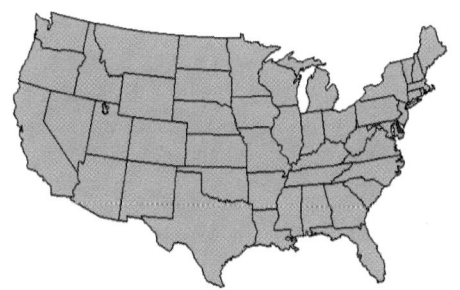

Anne Welsbacher
ABDO & Daughters

visit us at
www.abdopub.com

Published by Abdo & Daughters, 4940 Viking Drive, Suite 622, Edina, Minnesota 55435. Copyright © 1998 by Abdo Consulting Group, Inc., Pentagon Tower, P.O. Box 36036, Minneapolis, Minnesota 55435 USA. International copyrights reserved in all countries. No part of this book may be reproduced in any form without written permission from the publisher.

Published 1998
Printed in the United States of America
Second Printing 2002

Cover and Interior Photo credits: Allsport, Archive, Corbis-Bettman, Peter Arnold, SuperStock

Edited by Lori Kinstad Pupeza
Contributing editor Brooke Henderson
Special thanks to our Checkerboard Kids—Brandon Isakson, Priscilla Cáceres, Jack Ward

All population statistics taken from the 2000 census; U.S. Census Bureau. Other sources: *Delaware*, Fradin and Fradin, Children's Press, Chicago, 1994; America Online, Compton's Living Encyclopedia, 1997; World Book Encyclopedia, 1990.

Library of Congress Cataloging-in-Publication Data

Welsbacher, Anne, 1955-
    Delaware / Anne Welsbacher.
    p. cm. -- (United States)
    Includes index.
    Summary: Surveys the history, geography, and people of the small eastern state that was first to sign the United States Constitution.
    ISBN 1-56239-865-2
    1. Delaware--Juvenile literature. [1. Delaware.] I. Title. II. Series: United States (Series)
    F164.3.W37   1998
    975.1--dc21
                                                      97-15221
                                                        CIP
                                                        AC

Contents

Welcome to Delaware 4

Fast Facts About Delaware 6

Nature's Treasures 8

Beginnings 10

Happenings 12

Delaware's People 18

Big City, Small Towns 20

Delaware's Land 22

Delaware at Play 24

Delaware at Work 26

Fun Facts 28

Glossary 30

Internet Sites 31

Index 32

Welcome to Delaware

Delaware was the first state to join the United States. The first log cabins were built in Delaware. The country's first divided highway is in Delaware. And Delaware held the first beauty contest.

No wonder Delaware is called the First State! Delaware is very small. Only Rhode Island is smaller.

Delaware has beaches and hills. It has farms and **factories**. It has old houses and new buildings.

Delaware has many different things for such a small state. So Delaware also is called a "small wonder."

Opposite page: One of America's first log cabins was in Delaware.

Fast Facts

DELAWARE

Capital
Dover (32,135 people)
Area
1,933 square miles
(5,006 sq km)
Population
783,600 people
Rank: 45th
Statehood
December 7, 1787
(1st state admitted)
Principal river
Delaware River
Highest point
in New Castle County;
442 feet (135 m)
Largest city
Wilmington (72,664 people)
Motto
Liberty and independence
Song
"Our Delaware"
Famous People
Thomas F. Bayard, John Dickinson, E.I. du Pont, Howard Pyle

Delaware is one of the original 13 colonies

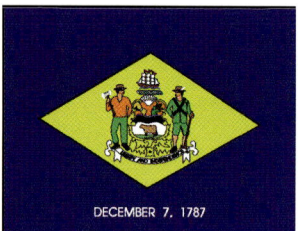

*S*tate Flag

*P*each Blossom

*B*lue Hen Chicken

*A*merican Holly

About Delaware
The Diamond State

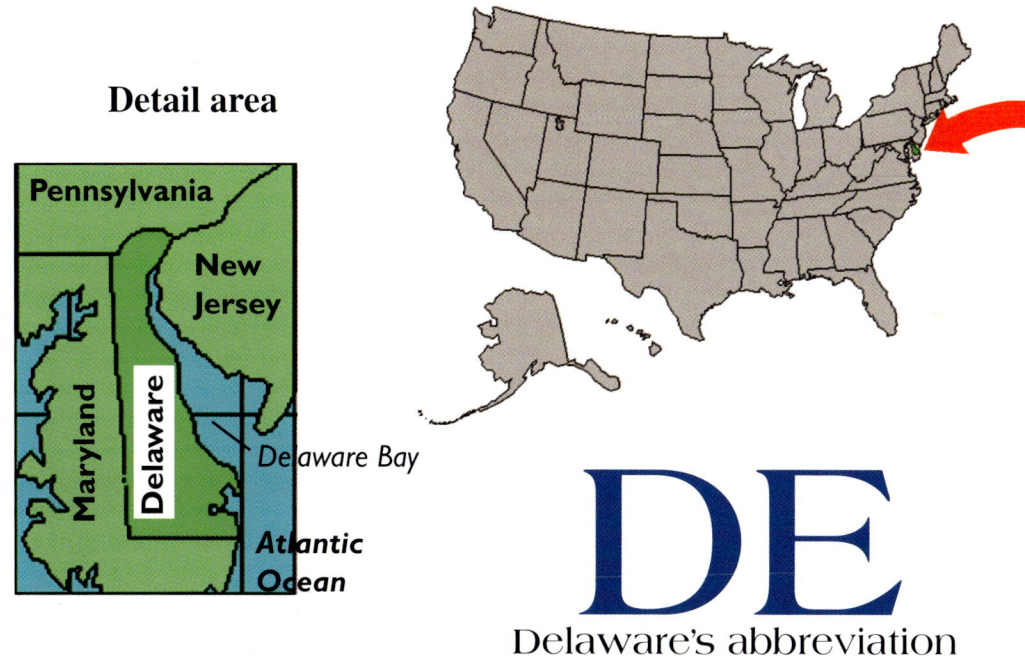

DE
Delaware's abbreviation

Borders: west (Maryland), north (Pennsylvania), east (New Jersey, Delaware Bay, Atlantic Ocean), south (Maryland)

Nature's Treasures

Most of the land in Delaware is good for farming. But it is a little sandy.

In some parts the soil is rocky. It has gravel, red sand, and **silt**. Silt is found near lakes and rivers.

Brandywine blue granite can be found in Delaware's soil. It is a pretty color. It is used for building things.

The weather in Delaware is mild. It is next to the ocean. The ocean cools the land in the summer. In the winter, the warm ocean water brings heat to the land.

Part of Delaware is not near the ocean. There, it is hotter in the summer and colder in the winter.

Opposite page: Delaware is near the Atlantic Ocean.

Beginnings

Early people in Delaware were called the **Lenni-Lenape**. Lenni-Lenape means "original people." The Lenni-Lenape lived in houses shaped like domes. In the 1600s, Dutch settlers came. Later, Swedish settlers came. The Swedish built the first log cabins in the United States.

Delaware was one of 13 English **colonies**. In 1776, **delegates** from the colonies met in Philadelphia. They voted on the Declaration of Independence. It said they would be a new country, the United States of America.

But some delegates didn't want to be a new country. The vote was a tie! Caesar Rodney, one delegate from Delaware, was very sick. But he rode all the way to Philadelphia just to vote. His vote broke the tie.

They fought the Revolutionary War with England. The colonies won. They became the United States of America.

In 1787, Delaware became the first state. It was the first to sign the United States **Constitution**.

In the 1800s, southern states wanted slavery. Northern states did not. Some southern states **seceded** from the United States. Delaware did not secede. But it had slavery until the end of the Civil War.

In the early 1800s, a powder mill was built in Delaware. The mill made gunpowder. Later, many **factories** grew in Delaware.

General George Washington at the Revolutionary War.

Happenings • Happenings • Happenings • Happenings • Happenings • Happenin

B.C. to 1600s

The First Delawareans

10,000 B.C.-1600s: People living in Delaware are the **Lenni-Lenape** and Nanticoke.

1609: Henry Hudson finds the Delaware **Bay** and Delaware River.

1600s: Early settlers from Holland and Sweden arrive.

ppenings • Happenings • Happenings • Happenings • Happenings • Happenings

Delaware
B.C. to 1600s

Happenings • Happenings • Happenings • Happenings • Happenings • Happenin

1700s

War Days

1700: Captain Kidd visits Delaware. Pirates attack along Delaware's shores in the late 1600s and early 1700s.

1776: Caesar Rodney signs the Declaration of Independence. His vote breaks a tie. The **colonies** become the United States of America.

1787: Delaware becomes the first state of the United States.

Happenings • Happenings • Happenings • Happenings • Happenings

Delaware
1700s

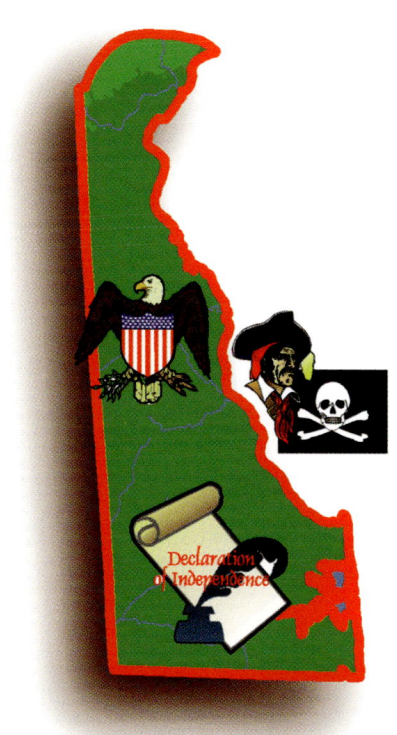

Happenings • Happenings • Happenings • Happenings • Happenings • Happeni

1800s to 1900s

New Times

1802: Du Pont builds a gunpowder **factory**. Later many more factories create things like paper and shoe leather.

1866: Quaker Thomas Kimber forms a group to build schools for black children and help people who were once slaves find jobs.

1911: America's first highway with a divider in the middle is built.

1900s: New companies create **chemicals**, fabrics, and cars.

1923: Mrs. Steele begins raising chickens as "broilers." Soon, Delaware is a leading state in raising chickens.

Happenings • Happenings • Happenings • Happenings • Happenings • Happenings

Delaware's People

Delaware is the second smallest state. There are 783,600 people living there.

The Nanticoke people still live in a small part of Delaware. Some people have family ties to the Dutch, Swedish, and English people who settled in Delaware.

There are people living there from other countries. But most Delawareans were born in the United States.

Annie Jump Cannon was born in Delaware. She **discovered** more than 300 new stars!

The whole du Pont family helped shape Delaware. The first du Pont came from France in 1800. He built a gunpowder **factory**. Du Pont had children and grandchildren and great-grandchildren. They still build factories and run companies.

Thomas Garrett, from Delaware, helped more than 3,000 slaves escape. Howard Pyle wrote *The Merrie Adventures of Robin Hood*. He was from Delaware, too.

Howard Pyle

Big City, Small Towns

Wilmington is the only big city in Delaware! Two out of every three people who live in Delaware live in New Castle County, the county where Wilmington is.

Many things are made in Wilmington. And because it is next to the ocean, some things are sent to other places around the world by boat.

Dover is the next biggest city. Dover is the capital of Delaware. Newark is the third biggest city.

Seaford and Rehoboth Beach are other towns.

Opposite page:
Wilmington, Delaware.

Delaware's Land

Delaware is shaped like a triangle with one flat side. Northern Delaware is mostly **urban**. Southern Delaware is mostly **rural**.

To the south and west of Delaware is Maryland. To the north is Pennsylvania. To the east is New Jersey and the Atlantic Ocean.

Delaware has two land areas. Most of the state has flat, low plains. Part of this area has **swamps**.

A small part in the north is called the Piedmont. The Delaware River runs from the Atlantic Ocean into the hills and valleys of northern Delaware.

Delaware has many forests. It has trees called beech, hickory, oak, loblolly pine, and wild cherry. Flowers that grow in Delaware are water lilies, magnolias, and pink lady's-slippers.

Delaware animals are deer, mink, otter, and foxes. It has blue herons, ducks, hawks, and hummingbirds. In its lakes and rivers are trout and catfish.

Next to the ocean shores are clams and oysters. And in the **swamps** are snapping turtles.

Trapp Pond State Park, Delaware.

Delaware at Play

Many people fish in Delaware. They catch big fish from the ocean. And families like to dig clams and hunt crabs in the Delaware **Bay**.

The Nanticoke Indian Pow-Wow is held in the fall. Also in the fall is the Delaware 500 Stock Car Race. Summertime events include arts, horse racing, and watermelons!

There are many museums and areas about history in Delaware. The Old Dutch House was built in the 1600s! Lewes and New Castle are areas with many old houses. Delaware has museums about art, farming, and animals, too.

Delaware also has state parks and forests. And you can see **bald cypresses** at the Great Pocomoke **Swamp**.

The Delaware 500 Stock Car Race is very popular.

Delaware at Work

Wilmington, Delaware, is called the "**chemical** capital of the world." Chemicals are the different parts in things, like the things in the air you breathe. Chemistry is putting parts together to make other things.

Here's a fun example of chemistry. Put cream, ice, sugar, and other things in a blender. Then mix them together. Soon you have ice cream!

Chemistry in the United States began in Delaware when a gunpowder **factory** was built in 1802. From that time on, many things using chemistry were made and **invented** there.

Things made in Delaware are chemicals, clothing, rubber, cars, and things made of metal.

Many farmers raise chickens. They also raise beef and hogs. And on some farms, holly is grown to make into wreaths at Christmas time.

Many ships come and go in Delaware **Bay**. They bring things in and carry them out. Boats also carry things on the Nanticoke River on the other side of the state.

Delaware has many chicken farms.

Fun Facts

- Christmas Seals came first to Delaware. Emily P. Bissell drew pictures on stamps. In 1907 the stamps were sold to make money to help cure a disease called tuberculosis.
- Only five states have fewer people than Delaware. They are Alaska, Vermont, Wyoming, and North and South Dakota.
- Delaware has no baseball teams. But many great baseball players came from Delaware. Some of them were John Joseph "Sadie" McMahon, and Victor Willia.
- The movie *Dead Poet's Society* was made in Delaware.
- At the Bombay Hook Migratory Waterfowl Refuge in Delaware, many different birds can be seen. The refuge covers 12 miles on the Atlantic coast. Every winter, when birds **migrate** south, they stop there to eat and rest.

Delaware has a waterfowl refuge.

Glossary

Bald Cypress: a kind of tree.
Bay: an area of the ocean near the land.
Chemicals: the parts in things; chemistry is putting the parts together to make other things.
Claim: to take.
Colony: a place that is owned by another country.
Constitution: a set of laws written by the people, not a king.
Delegate: a person who decides things for many other people.
Discover: to find for the first time.
Factory: a big building where things are made.
Invent: to make for the first time.
Lenni-Lenape: people who lived in Delaware in ancient times; the name means "original people."
Manufacture: the process of making something by hand or by machine.
Migrate: to move from one place to another. Birds migrate from the north to the south during winter.
Rural: in or near the country.
Secede: to break away.
Silt: the thick, muddy soil near the shore of a shallow river or lake.
Swamp: a muddy, grassy pond.
Urban: in or near a city.

Internet Sites

Delaware Direct
http://www.deldirect.com
Delaware Direct is Delaware's most complete and up-to-date source for statewide events, covering business, cultural, educational, and recreational attractions.

This site is subject to change. Go to your favorite search engine and type in Delaware for more sites.

PASS IT ON

Tell Others Something Special About Your State
To educate readers around the country, pass on interesting tips, places to see, history, and little unknown facts about the state you live in. We want to hear from you!
To get posted on ABDO & Daughters website E-mail us at "mystate@abdopub.com"

Index

A

animals 23, 24
Atlantic Ocean 22

B

bald cypress 24
beauty contest 4

C

chemicals 16, 26
colonies 10, 14
constitution 11

D

Declaration of Independence 10, 14
Delaware Bay 12, 24, 27
Delaware River 12, 22
delegates 10
Dover 20
du Pont family 18
Dutch settlers 10

E

English colonies 10

F

farming 8, 24
flowers 22
France 18

G

granite 8
gunpowder 11, 16, 19, 26

H

highway 4, 16

L

lakes 8, 23
Lenni-Lenape 10, 12
log cabins 4, 10

M

museums 24

N

Nanticoke 12, 18, 24
Newark 20

O

Old Dutch House 24
original people 10

P

Philadelphia 10
Piedmont 22
pirates 14

R

Revolutionary War 10
Rhode Island 4
rivers 8, 23
Rodney, Caesar 10, 14

S

secede 11
slavery 11
small wonder 4
summer 8, 24
Swedish settlers 10

W

Wilmington 20, 26
winter 8, 28

32